MW01599037

Liam,
The Next Gen Man.

Joke

better together*

*This book is best read together, grownup and kid.

 akidsco.com

a
kids
book
about

a kids book about

MASCULINITY

by Next Gen Men

a
kids
book
about

Text and design copyright © 2024
by A Kids Book About, Inc.

Copyright is good! It ensures that work like this can exist,
and more work in the future can be created.

All rights reserved. No part of this publication may be
reproduced, distributed, or transmitted in any form or
by any means, including photocopying, recording, other
electronic or mechanical methods, without the prior
written permission of the publisher, except in the case of
brief quotations embodied in critical reviews and certain
other noncommercial uses permitted by copyright law.
For permission requests, write to the publisher.

A Kids Book About, Kids Are Ready, and the colophon
'a' are trademarks of A Kids Book About, Inc.

Printed in the United States of America.

A Kids Book About books are available online: *akidsco.com*

To share your stories, ask questions, or inquire about bulk
purchases (schools, libraries, and nonprofits), please use
the following email address: *hello@akidsco.com*

Print ISBN: 979-8-89281-070-8
Ebook ISBN: 979-8-89281-071-5

Designed by Jelani Memory
Edited by Emma Wolf

Dedicated to Shaquille and Bryson.

You shone.

Intro

What does it mean to be a good man? How do we raise the next generation to be the curious, compassionate, and courageous young men the world needs today?

These days, a lot of people are talking about what masculinity means, but not enough of us are talking about it with young people themselves. At Next Gen Men, we believe that boys don't need to be taught to be true to themselves, support the people around them, or advocate for gender justice—they just need to be given permission.

This book exists to debunk the rigid cultural narrative about masculinity, and what it has meant to "be a man." We hope to encourage boys and masculine-exploring kids to figure out what masculinity means to them—even when it's hard.

And if you're a grownup reading this, well, that goes for you, too.

Masculinity is a story we tell ourselves, and one that is told to us.

In this book, I'll be telling you a story of masculinity from my perspective.

HI,

my name is Jonathon.

I love rock climbing.

I have a Siberian husky named Delta.

I know how to do a
backflip off of a swing set.*

I'm also very caring and gentle.

My favorite nail polish color is red.

I enjoyed ballet when I was a kid.

*Don't try this without a grownup's permission.

When I was growing up, a lot of people talked to me about masculinity...

and it wasn't always in nice ways.

A lot of the time what I learned about masculinity sounded like...

"GET BIGGER MUSCLES."

"TOUGHEN UP!"

"BOYS DON'T CRY."

"CUT YOUR HAIR, YOU
LOOK LIKE A GIRL."

"BOYS DON'T WEAR
NAIL POLISH."

The way I learned about masculinity could have been **OPEN** and **AFFIRMING**.

Instead, it was usually **CONTROLLING** and **HURTFUL.**

I was told that there was only 1 way
to be a boy—and that I was doing it

WRO

ONG.

I know now that we should be writing our own stories.

But it's something I didn't always know how to do.

And if you feel that way too, that's

OK!

The truth is that what it means to be a man can be a hard thing to figure out.

Many people have their own ideas about what masculinity should be.

I'm curious...what do you think of when you think of masculinity?

What do you think masculinity looks like? What does it sound like?

Turn to the person you're reading with and share what you're thinking about.

And then, ask them about masculinity when they were your age.

What did being a boy look like?

What were the stories they were told?

Are there similarities?

How about differences?

Here's the deal:

WHEN YOU WERE BORN, YOU ENTERED THIS WORLD AS AN AMAZING HUMAN, FULL OF POTENTIAL.

But way before you were born, without you being asked, all of these ideas and expectations existed about the kind of person you should be.

These ideas weren't based on your personal goals, loves, dislikes, or what made you happy.

They were formed based on made-up rules for only boys and girls.

Rules exist for many different reasons.

Some are really good, like how to respect the people around you or how to take care of your family pet.

But some rules exist just to create winners and losers.

This creates a divide between people.

And the catch with masculinity is that when we only follow rigid, unmoving rules about what it means to be a man,

EVERYONE LOSES—

including me and you.

Let me give you an example.

When I was your age, I liked to dance.

I took dance classes and practiced in my room.

I bought specific clothes to wear.

And then...my friends found out.

And they didn't think it
was as cool as I did.

They made fun of me,
and they laughed at me.

I understood loud and clear:

BOYS S
NOT
INTERES
DAN

SHOULD
BE
STED IN
NCE.

Long story short: I gave it up.

I lost a meaningful
form of self-expression.

My peers lost a sense of
trust with each other, that
we could all be celebrated
for our unique interests.

The world lost just a bit
of beauty and magic.

Oh, and one more thing.

When dance is seen as inappropriate for boys because it's something girls do, there's a bigger problem.

Because the meaning isn't just,
"You're a **BOY**, so don't be a girl."

It's also, "Girls are **INFERIOR**."

So even when the rules are about what boys can and can't do, girls and people of other genders lose out too.

I feel like there's a

BETTER

don't you?

WAY...

Not a world with winners and losers, but one where everyone has permission to be themselves.

What if...

THERE WERE NO RULES?!

What if masculinity wasn't 1 single thing that you were either doing "wrong" or doing "right," but rather something unique to you that you choose?

Your masculinity could be different from mine, from your neighbors', from your siblings', or from every person you know.

And that's a great thing.

Because if we get to write our own stories, we

can be a lot more than what we've been told.

Boys can be _____.

CREATIVE
FOCUSED
HUMBLE
CURIOUS
PATIENT

CAPABLE
RESILIENT
FLEXIBLE
STRONG
GENTLE

RESOURCEFUL
DETERMINED
SUPPORTIVE
BRAVE
LOVING
SENSITIVE
FORGIVING

FAIR
LOYAL
HOPEFUL
DEPENDABLE
EMPATHETIC
COMPASSIONATE
GENEROUS

HONEST
TRUSTING
THOUGHTFUL
EXPRESSIVE
CONFIDENT
ENTHUSIASTIC
MAGIC
FUN

INTROSPECTIVE
OPEN-MINDED
TRUSTWORTHY
PRESENT
GROUNDED
ACCEPTING
DECISIVE
GRATEFUL

We get to choose what masculinity means to us.

What does it mean to you?

Outro

You know the saying: boys will be boys. But boys will also become men. What if we stayed connected to boys and helped them become their best selves as they grow up?

In everything we do at Next Gen Men, one thing has always been clear: relationship is the medium through which all positive development takes place. This book will only help boys uncover their truest selves if they are held in steady, sensitive, and committed relationships by the people who matter most.

Grownups, that's on you. The young person next to you needs your time, your attention, and your affirmation. After all, boys will be... whatever we give them the space to be.

About The Author

Next Gen Men is a nonprofit organization changing the way we see, act, and think about masculinity. This book, like everything we do, was a collective effort.

Jake Stika (he/him) co-founded Next Gen Men in order to build a future in which boys and men experience less pain, and cause less harm. He's 6'8" and dedicated his younger life to basketball.

Jonathon Reed (he/him) works tirelessly to support the positive development of masculine-identifying youth, and designs resources and trainings for the parents, educators, and coaches who work alongside them.

Veronika Elyk (she/her) is an empathy-driven architect for men's grassroots involvement in the world of gender-based violence prevention and advocacy. She would move mountains for her beloved pitbull, Sarge.

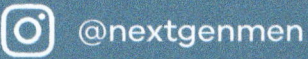 @nextgenmen   nextgenmen.ca

a kids book about MONEY
by Adam Stramwasser

a kids book about BEING INCLUSIVE
by Ashton Mota & Rebekah Bruesehoff

a kids book about diversity
by Charnaie Gordon

a kids book about LEADERSHIP
by Orion Jean

a kids book about IMMIGRATION
by MJ Calder

a kids book about SAFETY
by Soraya Sutherlin, CEM
in partnership with JUPF

a kids book about CLIMATE CHANGE
by Zanagee Artis & Olivia Greenspan

a kids book about IMAGINATION
by LEVAR BURTON

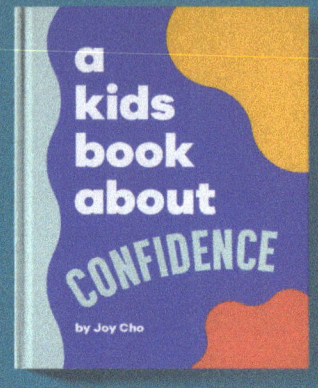
a kids book about CONFIDENCE
by Joy Cho

a kids book about S...

a kids book about ANXIETY
by Ross Szabo

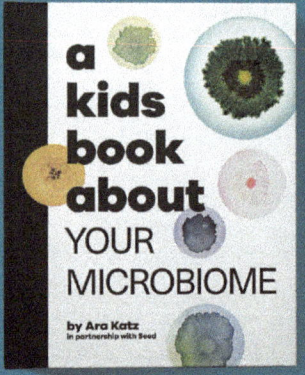
a kids book about YOUR MICROBIOME
by Ara Katz
in partnership with Seed

a kids book about racism
by Jelani Memory

a kids book about DISABILITIES
by Kristine Napper

a kids book about bor...
by KYLES

a kids book about DIVORCE
by Ashley Simpo

a kids book about cancer
by Dr. Kelsie Storm & Sarah Porter

a kids book about BEING TRANSGENDER
by Gia Parr
in partnership with The Gender Cool Project

a kids book about DEPRESSION
by Kileah McIlvain

a kids book a...

a kids book about shame...

a kids book about THE TULSA RACE MASSACRE

Discover more at akidsco.com

Printed in the USA
CPSIA information can be obtained
at www.ICGtesting.com
JSHW072001110924
69477JS00002B/4